# We Are the World
# We Are the Children

by the Students of Rutland Elementary School
Mt. Juliet, Tennessee

WRITE TOGETHER PUBLISHING
Nashville, Tennessee

Published by Write Together Publishing ™ LLC.
www.writetogether.com

ISBN 1-931718-29-6

Title: We Are the World, We Are the Children. Multiple authors.
Subject: Literary collections, poetry.

| | |
|---|---|
| Project Coordinator: | Joni Stone |
| Front Cover Art: | Autumn Bennett |

**For Write Together Publishing:**

| | |
|---|---|
| Publisher: | Paul Clere |
| Editor-in-Chief: | John D. Bauman |
| Art Director: | Bill Perkins |
| Publishing Coordinator: | Michael Pleasant |

---

# Dedication

This book is dedicated to Mr. Jim Slaughter, our guardian angel. Through his stories, he helped wake our imaginations. Through his actions and caring of others, we saw life as it should always be. Forever will he be fondly remembered as a friend and positive role model. May he live evermore through our stories, actions and caring for others.

# Table of Contents

## Making a Difference in the World

## We Are America



## When I Grow Up

## My Name Is

## Acrostics



## Friendship



## Menagerie

# Introduction

Reading is a fundamental life skill that should be a priority for every school and family. As a parent you should encourage your child to read, write, and create stories, poems, songs, cartoons, and illustrations that communicate a message to others. Reading should be done on a daily basis and should include opportunities for children to express themselves through questions and restatement of the main idea of the material being read. As you enjoy this book from our children, I hope you will thank the teachers and others who have encouraged and taught them to read.

Dr. Jim Duncan
Director of Wilson County Schools

# We Are the World

**W**orld peace is a dream of many.
**E**ven though we are alike in many ways,

**A**ll countries have differences.
**R**espect for all religions should be shown.
**E**vil hinders our way of life.

**T**errorist attacks around the world bring out
**H**eroes in many forms.
**E**verybody wants justice.

**W**ar is sometimes needed for justice and defense.
**O**ur country will stand tall as we
**R**eunite and join other countries to fight for
**L**iberty and justice for all.
**D**reams of world peace should never fade.
*Ashley Culbert*
*Ms. Buttrey's first grade class*

**W**orking together as a team, you will
**E**njoy whatever you're doing with better success.

**A**nswers to problems will come as a team and you'll
**R**eceive many rewards that will bring
**E**verlasting success.

**T**hink positive in everything you do. This will
**H**elp overcome any negative things and
**E**nd self-doubt.

**W**alk in the path of righteousness and
**O**bey the laws of the land and you will be
**R**ewarded.
**L**ove one another, and your
**D**ays will be filled with joy.
*Amber Myers*
*Mrs. Buttrey's first grade class*

**W**e want to play football.
**E**veryone play as a team.

**A** little baby cannot play football.
**R**uff giants cannot play football because they would step on the football players.
**E**very football player is nice, I hope.

**T**he football players better play nice.
**H**elp the football team make a tackle.
**E**ddie George plays football too.

**W**ork real hard
**O**r you will not win.
**R**un fast,
**L**ickity split
**D**og cat dog.
*Devin Boulogne*
*Ms. Buttrey's first grade class*

**W**orking together is good teamwork.
**E**ven if life throws you a curve ball, you just work a little harder to prove you can follow through.

**A**merica is the land of freedom and you should never forget it.
**R**espect yourself and others
**E**ven in the worst of times.

**W**hen the going gets tough, the tough get going.
**O**pen your heart to the world of wonders.
**R**emember that beauty is only skin-deep.
**L**ive life to the fullest always.
**D**on't ever say, "I can't." Can't never did anything!
*Mary Baldwin*
*Ms. Buttrey's first grade class*

**W**atching and learning from life
**E**xperiences.

**A**pplying myself and doing my best too.
**R**einforcing the important lessons.
**E**merging slowly into adulthood.

**T**ouching the people around me.
**H**elping make
**E**arth a better place.

**W**aving to every person.
**O**ffering my help to the elderly and
**R**especting everyone around me.
**L**ife is very important.
**D**o unto others as they do unto you.
*Tyler Cave*
*Ms. Buttrey's first grade class*

**W**e should be free.
**E**verybody does their exercises.

**A**mericans are we.
**R**espect God all the time.
**E**ach person is good.

**T**o be free is to be an American.
**H**elp other people.
**E**ating gives you energy.

**W**e live on Earth.
**O**ther people are important too.
**R**each for the sky.
**L**ove God and Jesus.
**D**o the right things.
*Logan Dillion*
*Ms. Buttrey's first grade class*

**W**e love Rutland Elementary School.
**E**veryone works together.

**A** lot of friends
**R**ealize success is important.
**E**veryone shares.

**W**e love the school.
**O**ne for all.
**R**utland is cool!
**L**isten to your teacher
**D**o your very best.
*Rachel Tichenor*
*Ms. Buttrey's first grade class*

**W**orking together
**E**njoying our differences

**A**s we
**R**espond to the
**E**ver changing world around us.
**T**eaching tolerance
**H**elping others
**E**njoying the freedoms of the great country.

**W**illing to go the extra mile for
**O**thers.
**R**eaching out to those
**L**ess fortunate as we
**D**evelop love for one another.
*Emily Cross*
*Mrs. Buttrey's first grade class*

**W**e have a special gift and that is education.
**E**ach child has this opportunity.

**A**s we grow, we learn.
**R**eading is growing.
**E**very day we learn and grow.

**T**he world is full of knowledge.
**H**ave faith in everything you do.
**E**very person is different.

**W**e need to love each other for individuality.
**O**ur society doesn't comprehend this.
**R**eaching our children at an early age can change this.
**L**ove everyone, every day, and learn from that.
**D**o the best you can, and no one can ask for more.
*Austin Nichols-Hurst*
*Mrs. Buttrey's first grade class*

**W**e are the future for today
**E**ncouraging each other along the way

**A**ccepting life's journey
**R**unning toward it with a smile
**E**njoying our peaceful lifestyle

**T**hinking of others.
**H**elping when we can
**E**ver giving a helping hand

**W**armness from our hearts
**O**ffers the gift of love
**R**eady to meet our goals
**L**earning how to do our best
**D**aily we show how we are blessed
*Katriel Coleman*
*Mrs. Buttrey's first grade class*

**W**onderfully created by God.
**E**verybody is made in his image.

**A**ll are brothers and sisters.
**R**eaching for guidance from above and
**E**njoying the journey along the way.

**T**ogether
**H**elping your neighbors
**E**njoying every day.

**W**e can serve
**O**thers with our talents and time.
**R**eaching out to those in need showing
**L**ove and kindness
**D**oing whatever our spirit guides us to do.
*Michaela Webb*
*Mrs. Buttrey's first grade class*

**W**e should love our world.
**E**verything in it is beautiful.

**A**lways keep it clean and
**R**emember to help others.
**E**very day, give someone a smile.

**T**he rabbit ran into his home.
**H**e got a bunch of carrots and gave one to
**E**very one of his friends.

**W**ill you be a friend
**O**f mine?
**R**emember it's good to be nice.
**L**ove your family.
**D**ad and Mom love our family.
*Lexi Emilia*
*Mrs. Buttrey's first grade class*

**W**ork hard
**E**very day at school.

**A**lways do your best.
**R**unning is fun.
**E**at all of your food.

**T**ake care of your parents.
**H**elp them all you can.
**E**ach day brush your teeth.

**W**ill you help me?
**O**ur class is the best.
**R**each for the sky.
**L**ove everyone.
**D**o only good things.
*Blake Word*
*Mrs. Buttrey's first grade class*

**W**ith help, we can do anything,
**E**ven write an

**A**crostic poem at
**R**utland Elementary School.
**E**ach of us is

**T**aught to do our best by
**H**elping others around us
**E**very day that we can.

**W**e are proud of ourselves if we help someone.
**O**ur world is the greatest world.
**R**eading books helps us
**L**earn to
**D**o our best.
*Dillon Kruppa*
*Mrs. Buttrey's first grade class*

**W**ork hard.
**E**verybody is special.

**A**lways try hard
**R**espect others
**E**njoy being a child.

**T**alents are gifts.
**H**elp each other
**E**xperience fun things.

**W**alk with pride.
**O**bey the rules.
**R**emember, you are special.
**L**ove one another.
**D**ream!
*Candis Corley*
*Mrs. Buttrey's first grade class*

**W**e are the Rutland Rockets.
**E**very child is loved here.

**A**ll our teachers care for us.
**R**espect is taught each day.
**E**ach and every one of us is friends.

**T**he teachers are so nice to us.
**H**appiness is here!
**E**xcellent lessons are taught.

**W**e love our teachers.
**O**h, if everyone were so lucky,
**R**utland would be their school.
**L**ook at all the fun we have.
**D**reams come true.
*Laura Bell*
*Mrs. Buttrey's first grade class*

**W**e are the future.
**E**veryone can succeed if they work hard.

**A**merica is our great country.
**R**ight choices make for a happy life.
**E**ven when we feel bad, a smile from a friend makes us happy.

**T**ime should not be wasted.
**H**appiness is the key to life.
**E**ach of us should love one another.

**W**e should always be kind.
**O**ur families are very important to us.
**R**eading helps us learn in school.
**L**ove for God, family, friends, and country makes us
a good person.
**D**reams can come true if we wish hard enough.
*Rylie Clairday*
*Mrs. Buttrey's first grade class*

**W**e love
**E**very child

**A**ll over the world.
**R**utland children are
**E**xtra special.

**T**rue friends make life
**H**eavenly
**E**ach day.

**W**hen we are kind to each
**O**ther, it makes a
**R**eal difference in the
**L**ives of everyone
**D**ay after day.
*James Taylor White*
*Mrs. Buttrey's first grade class*

**W**e are the future.
**E**veryone must come together.

**A**lways accomplish your goals.
**R**each your dreams in life.
**E**xpect the best from yourself.

**T**each others to love.
**H**elp each other.
**E**xcel in everything you do.

**W**e are the next leaders.
**O**ffer help to people.
**R**ealize that life is important.
**L**isten to each other.
**D**o your best to be patient, understanding, and loving to each other.
*Morgan Meade*
*Mrs. Buttrey's first grade class*

**W**illing to go the extra mile.
**E**veryone can lend a hand.

**A**lways treat others how you would like to be treated.
**R**emain true to yourself.
**E**njoy life to its fullest.

**T**ake the time to listen.
**H**elp those who can't help themselves.
**E**ncourage others to do their best.

**W**ith God all things are possible.
**O**ffering your best is all that is expected.
**R**espect is something everyone deserves.
**L**ive like there is no tomorrow.
**D**ecide to be an example, not a stumbling block.
*Bethany Stansell*
*Mrs. Buttrey's first grade class*

**W**hat will I do today?
**E**ach of us gets to decide.

**A**ll of us have a choice.
**R**ight or wrong,
**E**veryone gets to choose.

**T**rust yourself to make the right choice.
**H**ear your heart
**E**ven if you have to close your ears.

**W**hat did you choose?
**O**nly you know why.
**R**ight or wrong you decide your way.
**L**ive with your choice.
**D**id you choose to have a good day?
*Bryson Hutchison*
*Mrs. Buttrey's first grade class*

# We Are the Children

**W**e are *your* children.
**E**ncourage us with your understanding, trust and love.

**A**lways remember the blessings we are to each other.
**R**ead to us, talk to us, play with us, listen to us.
**E**njoy us while we are the youngest we will ever be again.

**T**each us and train us
**H**ow to be happy and how to be good citizens by your living
**E**xample.

**C**hildren aren't just little folks or young'uns. We are family... *we are you.*
**H**ow we behave and treat others
**I**s a reflection of how you are raising us.
**L**ove us always.
**D**ream with us, laugh with us, hurt with us, cry with us.
**R**eveal to us not only when we have disappointed you, but especially when we make you proud.
**E**nergize us often, because we have fewer responsibilities and can get bored easily.
**N**ever forget that *We are the World and We are the Children.*
*Steven York*
*Mrs. Faoro's first grade class*

**W**elcome to Rutland Elementary School.
**E**verybody is special.

**A**ll is special.
**R**each for the stars.
**E**xcellence in everything.

**T**eachers are good.
**H**aving Mrs. Kittrell is special.
**E**ach day we pray.

**C**ounting is fun.
**H**aving Mrs. Faoro is special.
**I** pay attention.
**L**ove everyone.
**D**oing our best.
**R**ising to the top.
**E**njoying our school.
**N**ow we've told you all.
*Dallas Karr*
*Mrs. Faoro's first grade class*

**W**orld
**E**veryone

**A**round
**R**outinely
**E**mptiness

**T**heir minds, and
**H**earts
**E**ntirely.

**C**hanging to begin
**H**elping
**I**ncluding our
**L**ove, hearts
**D**reams and always
**R**emembering peace
**E**ntirely in our hearts
**N**ever forgetting our world!
*Bradley Borders*
*Mrs. Faoro's first grade class*

**W**hen we are born
**E**verything is free.

**A**nd then we are told it is time for school.
**R**utland Elementary School is where I go.
**E**very day is a little hard.

**T**ake 2 from 7 add 5 makes 10.
**H**ours on the clock, cents on a dime.
**E**verything is still a little hard.

**C**an you believe it's August already?
**H**ere we go again.
**I**t's all the same people.
**L**aughing at friends, enjoying myself.
**D**imes in a dollar, minutes in an hour.
**R**emember that everything is a little easier.
**N**ow I am growing into a man. I can do it, I know I can.
*Cycle Bennett*
*Mrs. Faoro's first grade class*

**W**e are the children and with
**E**very passing day we

**A**re growing to be
**R**esponsible, respectful, and trustworthy individuals.
**E**very day we learn something new and

**T**omorrow is a new challenge.
**H**and in hand,
**E**ach of us will grow to

**C**herish each moment of our lives.
**H**appiness should not be
**I**gnored.
**L**ove, guidance,
**D**reams and running in the
**R**ain are dreams
**E**very child should explore.
**N**o one will dream the impossible dream.
*Sydney Parker*
*Mrs. Faoro's first grade class*

**W**e are the Rockets
**E**njoy each day.

**A**lways be nice.
**R**each for the stars.
**E**at lots of chocolate!

**T**ease your big brother.
**H**elp others.
**E**very day is a happy day.

**C**are for others.
**H**elp your parents.
**I** can take care of myself.
**L**isten to your teacher.
**D**o what you love.
**R**espect yourself.
**E**xpect great things of yourself.
**N**ever give up!
*Grace Smith*
*Mrs. Faoro's first grade class*

**W**e are the children of R.E.S.
**E**ach and every one of us is the best!

**A**sk anyone of us—
**R**utland Rockets we are true!
**E**very time you'll hear us cheer, "Go Green and Blue!"

**T**his is only my second year.
**H**elp me! Help me! Girls are here!
**E**verywhere I go, they suddenly appear!

**C**oming to school is so much fun,
**H**aving a blast learning 1+1!
**I**nteresting things happen in school.
**L**earning is fun and all too cool!
**D**ropping everything to read is so much fun.
**R**ecess and "happy news"—gotta getcha some!
**E**ventually it will be my time to leave.
**N**ever will I forget the memories!
*Shane St. John*
*Mrs. Faoro's first grade class*

**W**e stand up for what is right.
**E**ach child is loved by God.

**A**ll lives should be great.
**R**each for the stars.
**E**yes can see.

**T**each others about God.
**H**urt no one.
**E**ars hear things.

**C**haracter
**H**elps others.
**I**magination.
**L**ove yourself.
**D**reams.
**R**ealizing success is important.
**E**at healthy.
**N**ever hurt anyone!
*Clarie Brown*
*Mrs. Faoro's first grade class*

**W**e are the Rutland Rockets.
**E**ach one of us is special.

**A**lways love each other.
**R**emember to treat
**E**ach other as we would want to be treated.

**T**hank God for each day.
**H**opes and dreams can become true.
**E**verybody should like each other.

**C**hildren are our future.
**H**opes and dreams can become true
**I**f we try our best.
**L**ive well.
**D**o not get into trouble.
**R**emember to have patience.
**E**ncourage others.
**N**ever give up!
*Caleb Walpole*
*Mrs. Faoro's first grade class*

**W**hen I was a little boy,
**E**verybody was bigger than I.

**A**s I grew bigger I learned
**R**easons to be glad I was the youngest.
**E**verybody loved me.

**T**he youngest kid in the family
**H**as a lot to be thankful for.
**E**verybody wanted to help me as I grew.

**C**hristmas is special when you are the youngest.
**H**appiness is all around us.
**I**
**L**ove Christmas!
**D**on't you?
**R**emember that Jesus is the reason we celebrate
**E**very Christmas.
**N**ever forget it!
*Bobby Davidson*
*Mrs. Faoro's first grade class*

**W**inning isn't everything.
**E**veryone is special.

**A**lways be good.
**R**ealize success.
**E**verybody is caring to one another.

**T**ell the truth always.
**H**ave patience.
**E** is for effort.

**C**herish memories.
**H**elp one another.
**I** can help.
**L**ove one another.
**D**o your best.
**R**ealize your goals.
**E**stablish friendships.
**N**ever say never.
*Dillion Eakes*
*Mrs. Faoro's first grade class*

**W**ait your turn
**E**

**A**sk politely
**R**
**E**at with your mouth closed

**T**ake your turn
**H**
**E**

**C**
**H**ang up your coat
**I**
**L**
**D**
**R**emember to say thank you
**E**at your vegetables
**N**
*Joseph Walker*
*Mrs. Faoro's first grade class*

**W**illing to help others.
**E**ducation is very important.

**A**ll students are important.
**R**eading is fun.
**E**veryone can make a difference.

**T**eachers are special.
**H**appiness comes from inside.
**E**verything is possible if you try.

**C**hildren are the future.
**H**atred is the root of evil.
**I**f I could change the world I would.
**L**ife is a challenge.
**D**alton is my name.
**R**utland is the best school.
**E**verybody likes Mrs. Faoro.
**N**ever let anything keep you from reaching for the stars.
*Dalton Taylor*
*Mrs. Faoro's first grade class*

**W**here–
**E**ver I

**A**m, I will be
**R**espectful to
**E**veryone

**T**hat I meet
**H**ow–
**E**ver I

**C**an. I will
**H**elp teach all
**I**ndividuals to
**L**ove one another, to
**D**ance when they feel like crying and never to
**R**un in the face of adversity,
**E**ven in the darkness of
**N**ight.
*Sydney Palmer*
*Mrs. Faoro's first grade class*

**W**e help each other.
**E**veryone counts

**A**nd
**R**utland is our school where
**E**verybody is important.

**T**eachers are nice because they
**H**elp everyone.
**E**verybody is important.

**C**aring about each other and
**H**elping each other develop an
**I**nterest and a
**L**ove to learn.
**D**ays go by quickly because
**R**utland is fun.
**E**veryone is
**N**ecessary.
*Keanna Illgen*
*Mrs. Faoro's first grade class*

**W**ow!
**E**arthlings with energy to burn!

**A**sking lots of questions
**R**eading great books
**E**very day is a new adventure

**T**hinking up good stories
**H**appy smiles at recess
**E**ager to share ideas

**C**reative
**H**umorous
**I**nteresting
**L**ovable
**D**oers, not sitters
**R**emember us in your prayers
**E**veryone is a precious gift
**N**ever underestimate our potential!
*Dylan Jordan*
*Mrs. Faoro's first grade class*

**W**e
**E**at

**A**round the table and
**R**eally
**E**njoy

**T**ater tots. I like to
**H**elp
**E**verybody

**C**ook. I think
**H**aving food
**I**s important. I also
**L**ike to have
**D**ad
**R**ead stories to me
**E**ven though sometimes times I
**N**od off.
*Hunter VanCleve*
*Mrs. Faoro's first grade class*

**W**hen we all work together
**E**ach of us can make a difference.

**A**im for the top.
**R**each for the stars.
**E**xcel in whatever you do.

**T**ry your hardest.
**H**elp those who are in need.
**E**veryone can succeed.

**C**are for one another.
**H**old on to your dreams.
**I**'m proud to be an American
**L**iving in the best nation in the world.
**D**o the right thing.
**R**emember those who have died for our country,
**E**very soldier and civilian.
**N**ow is the time to stand tall.
*Kylie House*
*Mrs. Faoro's first grade class*

**W**e're the rockets from Rutland.
**E**very child tries hard.

**A**re all of the children getting AR points?
**R**ead your books and use your points to buy things.
**E**veryone gets kisses from Ms. DeeDee.

**T**he whole class got candy for being good.
**H**e ate his lunch while he was talking to friends.
**E**very day we learn something new.

**C**hoices you make now will help you in life.
**H**elp your friends.
**I**s everyone listening to the announcements?
**L**isten to your teachers.
**D**o your best and you will go far.
**R**edo your work and you'll do better.
**E**ven if you don't so well, you always get a second chance.
**N**ever give up, just do your best.
*Tori Gossett*
*Mrs. Faoro's first grade class*

**W**e are the world,
**E**verybody should know this.

**A**lways tell the truth.
**R**esponsibility to yourself and others.
**E**veryone should take care of the environment.

**T**reat others how you want to be treated.
**H**ave a heart.
**E**njoy life and your family.

**C**haracter counts.
**H**elp others in need.
**I**n the world all children are special.
**L**ove your family.
**D**on't be naughty.
**R**espect others.
**E**at healthy food.
**N**ever give up your dreams.
*Cameron Cheatham*
*Mrs. Brown's third grade class*

The world is full of children. This makes a happy world. I can give a gift of respect to all the children in the world.
*Knox Kelley*
*Mrs. Taylor's first grade class*

We may be small, we may not be tall, but that doesn't mean we are not alike in some ways. We are all a part of this world. I add happiness by being a girl.
*Avery-Ana Green*
*Mrs. Taylor's first grade class*

We are the world, we are the future. We are the light in our parents' eyes. We have the power over our future. No one has the power over us.
*Kassity Shepherd*
*Mrs. Brown's third grade class*

We are the same, we are the children. We children circle all over the world. Some help people. If someone drops their books, we should help pick them up. A lot of children don't even live in a house, but they never give up. I go to school and I live in a house, but it is still hard. I go to a good school. I go to Rutland Elementary School. I live in a well-built house, but I will never feel the pain other children feel. I live in the United States. If you are a citizen of the U.S., you are free. Some children are poor. They don't have eggs and sausage for breakfast. A lot of times they have to fight for their food.
*Derek Garcia*
*Ms. Ladas' third grade class*

What can I do as a child? I could put labels on the trash cans so that people don't get cut on something like glass and coke cans and plastic. People will not step on the trash and have to take a lot of baths. That way their water bills won't be so high. They can have more money to buy their food.
*Jasmine West*
*Ms. Ladas' third grade class*

One is less then two.
Three is less than four.
But children equals more.
*Linsey Ward*
*Ms. Ladas' third grade class*

We're the children of the world and we want to help those who are sick, poor, and homeless. I'm a child made with God's only power. We may look alike but we're not. We're different from everybody. We're the same on the inside and we're different on the outside. Best of all, I'm glad I live in America!
*Kati Pierce*
*Ms. Ladas' third grade class*

We are the children of the world. We have different colored eyes and different colored hair. Some of us play sports, some do not. We might be blind, we might be deaf. We may be teenagers or kids. But after all the differences, we're still the same. We are still the children of the world.
*Kyle Illgen*
*Mrs. Brown's third grade class*

There are many reasons why I like being a child in our world today. You can still play with toys. You don't have to worry about going to war. You can do fun stuff like riding roller coasters. You can play with toys every day that you are free, or you can study. You don't have to go to war to fight. You can still ride roller coasters.
*Katrina Bald*
*Mrs. Lovin's fourth class*

There are many reasons why I like being a child in our world today. Some of those reasons are having enough time to dream about the future and not having too much responsibility. To dream takes a lot of planning. Being a kid, I have a lot of time to take certain lessons and set goals.
*Abby Kanak*
*Mrs. Lovin's fourth grade class*

I know I'm just a kid, but I can still help the world. I can pick up trash or I can just mow someone's yard. I can go buy groceries for old people. I help my mom around the house. I'm to young to donate blood, but I can donate money to the Red Cross.
*Jamie Collins*
*Mrs. Cardwell's fourth grade class*

We are the children, we are the world, we are the United States, which is united. We are the people. We are the world. We will fight to have our freedom! We are the kids. We are the world. We will believe in God, pray and thank Him for the things that He has done for us!
*Angelica Santiago*
*Mr. Byrd's fifth grade class*

We are the children
of the world.
We pray every day,
and hear God's
voice.
Our choice is,
we are the
world.
We are the
children.
Pray to God
every day.
Anywhere, every place,
Pray, pray.
God, our Father,
Bless the children
of the world.
*James Flatt*
*Mrs. Hall's fifth grade class*

We are the children who live among the free and brave.
Others who are homeless, or in danger, we try to save.
This land is our home, peaceful it shall stay,
Hoping to greet other people who want to live where they may.
Hopefully you see my side of the story
And will bring many people glory.
It is not only important to me,
But to all of the land of the free!
*Amber Hood*
*Mrs. Hall's fifth grade class*

There is love in this world. Love comes from families and children. Parents think children are the best thing in the whole world. But only one thing is not good in this world. That is how some people are poor and don't have homes. It is very sad how people are poor and don't have food and water to clean themselves. Some children and adults don't think of people that have nothing while they have everything. Children are the whole world, but people need to care about others that have nothing. People who are poor can starve and that is not a good thing. When some people starve they can die. This world has a lot of kids who have never, ever seen toys, beds,

food, or anything like that. Children are this world, even those who are poor. Many people feel they did a good thing to help poor people. But most of all they helped their children become more responsible.
*Courtney Swanson*
*Ms. Lynn's fifth grade class*

We are the world,
A world of many different races,
A world of many different places.
We are the children.
Some of us are short and some are tall.
Some of us are big and some are small,
We are the children,
We are the world.
*Kati Farthing*
*Mrs. Hall's fifth grade class*

We are the children of the world. We understand things that people think we don't. After the attack in September, everyone has united, even the children. Since everyone has united, we have learned more about each other. We have also learned more about each other's families. We have learned that children have lost family members and how they feel about that. Most of all, we learned more about our country and now we understand!
*Samantha Eldridge*
*Mrs. Miller's fifth grade class*

We are the children of the world,
We are proud of the ones before us.
We are the love and hope of our great country.
We will protect the land we live on.
We will protect our great country's pride.
We love our home more than any other.
We will help make the future better.
Will you help?
*Katie Buck*
*Mrs. Miller's fifth grade class*

I saw a child with problems in this world and I wanted to help him out. I went to talk to him and he told me that his family didn't have any money. Then I thought of something. I told the child that I was going to talk to my dad. He helped the boy's dad out by loaning him some money. That's what our world is about—helping each other. My family and I helped the children's family.
*Richard Martinez*
*Ms. Lynn's fifth grade class*

We are the world.
We are the children.
We will make a difference
By treating everyone the same,
No matter the race or religion,
No matter from what country they came.
We will all stand tall
And show respect to all.
God bless the children everywhere.
*Jillian MacDonald*
*Mrs. Miller's fifth grade class*

We are the world,
We are the children.
Although we're small,
We come in millions.
Our lives are changing
Every minute and every day.
We try and help in every way.
We are the children of the world,
Boys and girls.
We're all the same.
*Kaitlyn Baker*
*Mrs. Miller's fifth grade class*

We are the world, we are the children and
*The world is changing.*
Every minute and every second and every day
*The world is changing.*
Life is cut short every minute and second
*The world is changing.*
Like on September 11, 2001, the bombing changed the world
*The world is changing.*
We are the boys and girls of the world and
*We are all changing.*
*Jordan Sanders*
*Mrs. Miller's fifth grade class*

# Making a Difference in the World

Flags make the world pretty.
*Hayden Bramble*
*Mrs. Kirby's kindergarten class*

The blue river makes the world beautiful.
*Samantha Burnett*
*Mrs. Kirby's kindergarten class*

I love the world because we have Halloween.
*Kameron Shepherd*
*Mrs. Kirby's kindergarten class*

My mom and I were dancing around the world.
*Virginia Kelley*
*Mrs. Kirby's kindergarten class*

I like my house.
*Riley Bass*
*Mrs. Kirby's kindergarten class*

I put the seed in the flower.
*Emma Ginter*
*Mrs. Kirby's kindergarten class*

I would shape the world into a heart.
*Sarah DeRosett*
*Mrs. Kirby's kindergarten class*

I love the world because it has rivers. I would change the river to a dam.
*Jake Lefler*
*Mrs. Kirby's kindergarten class*

The world is pretty every day.
*Morgan Goodwin*
*Mrs. Kirby's kindergarten class*

The world has tornados.
*Drew Wiggins*
*Mrs. Kirby's kindergarten class*

I will help the world by being a four-wheel driver. I would carry people in a wagon if they were hurt.
*Cody Glover*
*Mrs. Sloan's kindergarten class*

I will help the world by being a singer. I can make people happy.
*Dylan Cheatham*
*Mrs. Sloan's kindergarten class*

I would help the world by being a horse trainer. I would be helping horses which are a part of the world.
*Darby Rutledge*
*Mrs. Sloan's kindergarten class*

I will help the world by being an airplane pilot. I would take people to another airplane place.
*Cameron Reddick*
*Mrs. Sloan's kindergarten class*

I would help the world by being a teacher. I would teach kids how to know about the world.
*Amelia Smith*
*Mrs. Sloan's kindergarten class*

I like school. School is all about reading. School is fun.
*Alex Russell*
*Mrs. Faoro's first grade class*

God is always watching the world. He makes magic come down and picks you up when you're dead.
*Tyler Hayzlet*
*Mrs. Kirby's kindergarten class*

More grapes!
*Michaela Micco*
*Mrs. Kirby's kindergarten class*

I can be part of the world to make it a better place. I can be proud of myself if I have good character.
*Dana Holt*
*Mrs. Taylor's first grade class*

If I could change the world, I would recycle the trash that the people throw on the grass. And I would help the Army because they help us.
*Nora El-Chaer*
*Mrs. Elder's second grade class*

If I could change the world, I would change it so that we could do whatever we want and not have school.
*Seth Wofford*
*Mrs. Elder's second grade class*

If I could change the world, I would make it so clean and I would show a lot of respect to other people. And they would have lots of toys.
*Dylan Lannom*
*Mrs. Elder's second grade class*

If I could change the world, I would help the sick and give kids food. I would help the world be a better place and have peace and stop wars.
*Deanna Jenkins*
*Mrs. Elder's second grade class*

If I could change the world, I would help kids find new houses. If I could I would try to clean up all of Tennessee. When I grow up I will help the sick.
*Jesscia Estes*
*Mrs. Elder's second grade class*

If I could change the world, I would make sure everybody had food.
*Ty Smith*
*Mrs. Elder's second grade class*

If I could change the world I would be Like Dr. Martin Luther King, Jr. Dr. King spent his life fighting for the rights of other people. Today Americans can remember Dr. King on the third Monday in January. If I could change the world, I would stop pollution and killing.
*Darrell Holt*
*Mrs. Elder's second grade class*

If I could change the world there would be peace on earth. We would win the war and stop litter. America fights back!
*Tyler Binkley*
*Mrs. Elder's second grade class*

If I could change the world I would save mountain gorillas and make sure all are safe. I would make sure none are killed, and make sure they have plenty of food.
*Laurel Everett*
*Mrs. Elder's second grade class*

If I could change the world I would give food and toys and other things to the poor so they would feel like they were at home.
*Sydney Vanlandingham*
*Mrs. Elder's second grade class*

If I could change the world I'd try to stop wars from happening. I'd try to get the homeless people some food and homes to live in.
*Kalli Crowell*
*Mrs. Elder's second grade class*

I would pick up the trash. I would help the people who are having trouble. I would send money to the poor people. I would take care of this world.
*Danielle Booth*
*Mrs. Pryor's second grade class*

I would plant good and fresh flowers. Do you think I should plant flowers? I can make the world better by cleaning up and making habitats for the animals.
*Mikka Maderal*
*Mrs. Pryor's second grade class*

Do not throw trash on the ground. Try to keep the world clean. Make sure there are no bullies in the world.
*Ryan Engel*
*Mrs. Pryor's second grade class*

No work.
*Cassie Bean*
*Mrs. VanCleve's second grade class*

I will stand up for someone, and if someone gets hurt I will help them. I hope everyone has a good character. Everyone is special!
*Melissa Woodruff*
*Mrs. Brown's third grade class*

There are millions of ways that we can help people and children in other countries. We can help them by giving gifts, money, toys for the children, books, and clothes. Canned goods would be cool too. If you go to church they'll probably do the same thing.
*Kylee Glass*
*Ms. Ladas' third grade class*

Did you know that kids all over the word need help from their moms and dads? Some need money, some need food, some need clothes, some need games to play. Some need a home to live in. Some people in America, Mexico and China need a home. Thousands of people need homes, food, toys and clothes. Some don't go to school that really need help. Moms need help taking care of their babies. I am glad to have a home and all that I need to live.
*Cayla Corley*
*Ms. Ladas' third grade class*

We could help the children in other countries by giving them food if they don't have food to eat. We could give them water if they don't have water to drink. If they don't have clothes, we could give them clothes to wear. I know God loves everybody and they love Him. I want everybody to have freedom.
*Danielle Chaffin*
*Ms. Ladas' third grade class*

A lot of people like America like I do. A lot of people like New York like I do. A lot of people like China like I do. A lot of people like school like I do. People all like friends.
*Steve Workman*
*Ms. Ladas' third grade class*

People in America are not the same as other people in different countries. In some countries, people don't have anything to drink or eat, and the children don't have medicine when they are sick. They don't have toys or anything to play with. They don't know how to read because they don't have anyone to teach them. They don't know how to write. I know how to write because someone teaches me.
*Alex Ward*
*Ms. Ladas' third grade class*

I really love this world and I have taken good care of it. I am thankful for the water and the life God has given us on this earth. I am also thankful for the food and the good old United States of America. I want everyone to have an open mind and a good life.
*Zach Selby*
*Mrs. Laster's third grade class*

Our world is good. Not everybody is good, some are mean. That is not good and I don't like it. I don't want the war anymore, but America is going to win the war. I just know it. I want to try to start to be nice because I don't want any bad people on this earth. I only want good people on earth because I don't want anyone to get hurt. I love America because it is very safe for me. I like my house because it's warm, it has big rooms, it has nice cabinets, it has nice bathrooms, and the sinks and the showers work well. It has nice carpets and it has a lot of space. America is a wonderful place.
*Kayla Clark*
*Mrs. Laster's third grade class*

I don't like what is going on in this world with the war and the people that have died. I don't want to see anyone in front of me because it makes me sad. I'm glad that people like me because I like them too. I'm proud to be an American.
*Jessica Tallent*
*Mrs. Laster's third grade class*

We should try to be good citizens. Keep the world clean. Teach your children good things, not bad things. Don't talk back to your elders. Be good to people. I think war is a bad thing because if you fight in a war, people can get killed. Don't kill so you don't go to jail. Some people are good on the inside, so why are some other people bad? Try to be good people.
*Drew Chester*
*Mrs. Laster's third grade class*

Our world is not a perfect place because we take our country for granted. We also pollute our water, air and our planet. We do not recycle, we litter. We break laws, but our country is very strong. We stick together even when we are in a war. Our troops are very strong. We are going to win this war. Do you think we're going to win? I know we're going to win because we are strong when we need it the most. Our country is very strong when we stick together but we are weak when we pull apart. Now we need to stick together!
*Patrick Cashman*
*Mrs. Laster's third grade class*

Dear World,

We can make our world a better place by picking up trash, recycling, and being a good citizen. We should be thankful for what we have that other people don't have.

We are the world and we can be nice to others. We are the children who live in this world to have freedom. People have good in them if they can just find it. Other countries don't have freedom. We should appreciate the freedom we have.

Please help our world become a better place.

Love,
Marissa

*Marissa Valenzuela*
*Mrs. Laster's third grade class*

The world is the best. We are part of the world. When I grow up I want my kid to be good. The world is the most wonderful place. The whole wide world is a friend to me. I love the world because God made it.
*Brandon Long*
*Mrs. Laster's third grade class*

To make the world a better place, I can care for others. We should all love each other. Elderly people that are in nursing homes can't be home for the holidays, so I can visit them and I can send them cards since their families are not there. I can donate money to the poor and food for the homeless. People in Afghanistan are not allowed to come out of their houses, go to school, read, or learn, so I could help the people of Afghanistan. Everybody needs to be thankful for what they have. I can help crippled people, challenged people, and paralyzed people, because everybody needs friends and I could be their friend. Soldiers in the U.S. Army have families at home, but they can't be with them because they are helping other people. I can show courtesy for other people and be nice, rather than mean. I have a responsibility to be respectful of other people.
*Jordan Stewart*
*Mr. Marczak's third grade class*

I would make everyone have the same amount of money and make everything in the world free. Then, nobody would rob banks or break into houses to steal other people's stuff. It would stop people from killing each other and people would not get mad because they wanted something someone else had. If you wanted to go to Disney World, you could at any time. I could get a cool car like a Dodge Viper and a motorcycle for my brother, my dad, and me. Then, everyone would be happy because they would have whatever they wanted and nobody would fight. That's what I would do, and that would change the world.
*Tyler Harper*
*Mr. Marczak's third grade class*

The reason I like this world is because we have peace and I love the environment. I'm glad we have food to survive and I am thankful for my family. We don't pollute. We protect our earth.
*Cody Campanali*
*Mr. Marczak's third grade class*

To make the world a better place, I could give homeless people homes and give them food to eat because they might die on the streets. I can let homeless people take showers in my bathroom so they can keep themselves clean. I could water plants so that they can stay alive and we can breathe. I could clean up trash in my community so that it will be clean. I could keep my streets clean so that they won't look trashy, because littering is bad for animals, people, and the whole world. Putting trash in a trashcan, not on the floor, is good because your brothers or sisters might get sick and die if trash were left all around. Trash belongs in a dumpster.
*Chris Williams*
*Mr. Marczak's third grade class*

The world has too much trash. Everyone should try to recycle. I can recycle paper, plastic, cans, materials, trees, tires, computers, and garbage to make fuel. I can help homeless people get homes. I can help people that might be living on the streets. I can cut tall grass so that people can see over the grass and there won't be so many car wrecks. We don't need terrorists. A world with terrorism is terrible, so we need to catch terrorists so that we will have a better world.
*Jesse Brown*
*Mr. Marczak's third grade class*

I could volunteer to help people carry their groceries. I could also help others by teaching how to be kind. I could help save paper by recycling. I wish people would not pollute because it is bad for the Earth. I could also clean up trash for the Earth to make it not look messy, because the Earth does not deserve to be treated like that. I could help someone in need by giving them food or drinks. I could help a needy family by giving them money. I could help the world by visiting every state and cleaning up trash so that others can see a clean world.
*Zachary Gray*
*Mr. Marczak's third grade class*

I can make the world a better place by giving the homeless some canned foods, clothes, shoes, and money so they will be happy. I could recycle paper so that we do not have to cut down trees, which help us breathe. I can help educate people about not polluting the ocean so fish and other animals that live in the ocean will not die. I can help stop trucks that let smoke out of their exhausts that pollute the air. I can help people not do drugs so it won't mess with their lungs and kill them.
*Autumn Mitchell*
*Mr. Marczak's third grade class*

I think to make the world a better place, you must volunteer your time. There are a lot of ways to make the world better. Some ways are to recycle things like aluminum, paper, glass, plastic, and cloth. Another way is to go to a public place, such as a park or a neighborhood, and pick up trash. I could go to a local homeless shelter and give my time to those who aren't capable of helping themselves. I could also help my neighbors by helping them bring in groceries or taking out the trash. Those are ways I can make the world a better place.
*Cheyenne Biggs*
*Mr. Marczak's third grade class*

I can make the world a better place by building homes for poor people so they can keep warm. To make the world a better place, people can adopt babies that need homes and parents. I can help people make the choice not to take illegal drugs, so that they throw them away, not take them and do stupid things.

If there are any poor kids, I could give them toys to play with. I could give some of my stuff to the poor for Christmas and all the holidays too, because people need to feel happy for special times of the year. I could also help the poor people go to school to learn so they can make money and take care of their families.
*Sharahd Stinson*
*Mr. Marczak's third grade class*

I could make the world a better place by volunteering to help clean the park and streets so animals can have homes, not a piece of paper for a nest. When we litter, it causes lots of problems for people and animals. It's sad that people have to litter when they can't find a trashcan to put their trash in. Throwing litter on the ground makes animals live a bad life because they would be living in trash. If there is too much trash, they can't get food because the Earth is polluted and so is their food. Without food, all the animals would die.
*Shane Meadows*
*Mr. Marczak's third grade class*

People in America are not all the same, and not all children are the same. Some kids are Spanish. I hope the world does not get worse then it already is. America is the best in the world. That's what I think.
*Josh Brown*
*Mrs. Ladas' third grade class*

There are some people who have nothing. My mom last year gave the poor one hundred dollars because she cared about them. My mom gives twenty dollars on regular days, but on holidays she gives people a lot of money like a hundred dollars. My sister gave me a teddy bear, but I told my mom that I wanted to give my teddy bear away to the poor. I felt bad and felt inside that I should.
*Sara Ginter*
*Ms. Ladas' third grade class*

I think we need to keep the world clean and nice. The way the world is now is trashy and dirty. That's not good. If we work together we can clean the world and make it a nice and clean for people and animals. One day when we work together, the earth will be clean. If you were me, you'd know how I feel. If you just get a trash bag and clean the earth, it would be much better.
*Emily Madewell*
*Mrs Laster's third grade class*

I could help the world by giving kids who don't wear shoes my own shoes. I could help the world by collecting money for the poor. I could help the world by starting a church in another country and teaching Bible stories about Jesus Christ, the Son of God. I could be a Sunday school teacher. I could be a singer and sing about God. I could put on puppet shows or plays about God.
*Jamie Cates*
*Mrs. Cardwell's fourth grade class*

I can do things for the environment such as picking up trash or mowing people's lawns for money for charity. I can do things for other people such as helping an old person cross the road, holding the door for a person who is in a wheelchair and giving money to charity. I can have a car wash and wash the cars for donations. I can walk somebody's dog. I can rake all the leaves out of somebody's yard if they are on vacation or away. I can take care of somebody's dog if they are not home.
*Josh Eldridge*
*Mrs. Cardwell's fourth grade class*

You would not think kids can do much about what is going on in our country and everywhere else. I am too young to donate blood to the Red Cross, but I can have a car wash and donate all the money to the Red Cross. I think that is as good as giving blood. I could also pick up litter to help the environment. I could have a food drive to feed the poor and the people whose homes were damaged in New York. Kids can do a lot.
*Sara Tichenor*
*Mrs. Cardwell's fourth grade class*

I can help old people by helping them cross the street, carrying heavy groceries, taking care of them, making sure they take their pills, and driving them to the doctor. I could also drive them to the grocery store and back home.
*Jenny Easterling*
*Mrs. Cardwell's fourth grade class*

I can help improve the world by keeping it clean and beautiful. I could pick up trash and recycle. I could also plant flowers and trees. One more thing I can do is protect the environment. We can help others by giving things to Good Will. One last way we can help is to give at Christmas through Operation Christmas Child and Angel Tree. That's how we can improve the world.
*Emily Buck*
*Mrs. Cardwell's fourth grade class*

I can help the world by picking up trash and by recycling the trash I pick up. I could raise money for the homeless. I could start a non-violence committee. I could do something for a group of people, then the group of people that I helped would help another group of people so it would never stop. Or I could just be a nice person. This is my way to start.
*TJ Preston*
*Mrs. Cardwell's fourth grade class*

To make the world better, you should pick up trash. We should have police at every store. We should have a park ranger at every park. Do not steal. Do not kill. Do not make fun of anybody. Love the world. Do not judge people by how they look
*Jordan Lee*
*Mrs. Bennett's fourth grade class*

To make the world a better place, we should pick up trash, make more friends and go to church. If everybody does these things, everybody will have a good life. Do not kill. Do not steal. Do not make fun of anybody. Do not judge people by how they look. Love your world.
*Zane Vanlandingham*
*Mrs. Bennett's fourth grade class*

I can help the world by not littering and not smoking, which both cause pollution. I could pick up trash. Since I am nine years old, I cannot give blood, but if I were old enough, I would. My mom and Gram gave blood to the Red Cross, which I thought was really nice.
*Katie Groves*
*Mrs. Cardwell's fourth grade class*

I hope you can help! Come on, people, help me stop the war and not have burglars in the neighborhood. Please, people, help me stop the bad people. Be nice and be thankful to people. They will proudly do the same thing to you. I will too.
*Dalton Steele*
*Mrs. Bennett's fourth grade class*

If I could change one or two things about the world, I would stop war and warfare. I would make sure everyone was treated the same. In this country, we have many freedoms, like the freedom of opinion and freedom of speech. I think we should all be fair and equal.
*Skylar Stone*
*Mrs. Bennett's fourth grade class*

I would give food and give clothes to people who need them. I might even give my new stove. I would teach the Bible to people and tell them about how God loves them. Help me to help them too.

So remember, when you are walking down the street and you see someone homeless or beat, remember the golden rule by being kind to others and they will be kind to you.
*Jai Crowder*
*Mr. Byrd's fifth grade class*

Our world is always changing and so are the people in it. If I could change the world, many things would be a lot easier! First, I would get people to help stop world hunger. Next, I would educate people in order to help them realize how important our rain forests and animal species are. After that, I would help people who lost other people and people who lost their homes or are homeless. Also, I would let everyone know that they are loved and should get along with everyone else. That way, there would be no crime or wars. I always wonder why people fight and argue so much and don't realize that God made the Earth for us all to love each other. We all could save the world if we help each other be happy, caring, and thankful. Finally, if you want to save your earth, do all you can! Don't do it alone. Start with one thing and be careful. Most of all, enjoy life while you have it. My mom always says, "Gather ye rosebuds while ye may!"
*Jessica Jenkins*
*Mrs. Hall's fifth grade class*

If I were the ruler,
I would do everything just to make the world right.
I would do everything I could
To make the world bright.
I would try to make the world be a light.
A light to freedom, no weapons to kill,
No money to bill.
The past is just a dream.
My life is an old theme.
I would take time to think about others
And save a lot of lives too.
Dreaming is done,
That would be fun.
Now back to my life,
That fun life I always knew.
*Cheyenne Swift*
*Mrs. Hall's fifth grade class*

If I ruled the world, I would have no weapons or things like weapons. I'd refuse to use brute strength, and all the bombs that are left I'd defuse.

So be noble, upright and mobile, for the world is full of the unexpected and more is yet to come.
*Adam Banach*
*Mr. Byrd's fifth grade class*

People of the world are like friends. They can take you to the very end. Some of them are nice and angry but they can also be very cranky. I see the people all around me. It's like they are jumping around me. People of the world will always be unique.
*Justyn Mitchell*
*Mrs. Hall's fifth grade class*

Kids can make a difference. If you don't believe it, try it and see what you can do. Some can be president, some can be policemen and some can be elite forces. When kids try to make a difference, they usually succeed. See if you can make a difference.
*Jace Smith*
*Mrs. Miller's fifth grade class*

If I could change the world,
I would make it a better place.
There would be no terrorism
Or even hate against another race.
People would live and not die.
Mothers would laugh and not cry.
If I could make the world a better place,
Everyone would have a smile on their face.
*Sean Ray*
*Mr. Byrd's fifth grade class*

If I ran the world, I would take all the mean people and put them in one state and let them hurt each other. Then I would take all the nice people and let them have nice homes and nice cars. Then there would be a peaceful world. I would stop the war and help New York to be safe again.
*Zach Begley*
*Ms. Lynn's fifth grade class*

I wish the whole world had peace,
So we wouldn't have terrorists, so to speak,
Because if we had peace, nobody would fight,
And there would be no war in sight.
You could look for miles and see no gunshot,
Except maybe a hunter and that's not a lot.
If there were peace, all the countries could unite.
That way nobody would need to fight.
Then nobody would live at risk,
And there would be no terrorists.
*Michael Putman*
*Mr. Byrd's fifth grade class*

If I could change the world, I would give all the orphans in the world moms and dads that love them very much. I would let all the homeless people have homes. Everyone should have food, shelter and clothing. We all deserve something in the world. We are all the United States of America and have freedom and equal rights. Let's keep it that way now and forever.
*Whitney Goodwin*
*Ms. Lynn's fifth grade class*

In some countries, they have no food to eat
And no shoes for their feet.
There are no toys
For the girls or boys.
When Christmas comes they have no joy.
When night comes they have no beds
Or pillows for their heads.

In our country, when a holiday comes there is a lot of play
And we say, "Hooray!"
We have plenty of food and drinks
And schools to make us think.
Our country has great pride
That no one can divide.
*Billy Dull*
*Ms. Lynn's fifth grade class*

When I am president, I will not only change America, I will change the whole world. I will change the world by saving it. I will get everybody to pick up the trash and plant new trees, saving the environment. When I am president, I will tell the builders not to tear down any more trees to build houses. If they don't stop, they will be put to jail. I will tell them that I am serious about this because our world is going through a lot of destruction, and some of it is caused by us. I want to help people get along with each other. If people don't get along we will put them on a spaceship and send them to Mars to stay. So let's help the world by saving it, not destroying it. When I am president, I will not only help the U.S.A. but I will also help the world by saving it. That's what I will do when I am president.
*Jackie Marks*
*Ms. Lynn's fifth grade class*

Violence. It's what we hear about every day on the news, in the papers, even sometimes at school. It scares us all that maybe one day something just might happen to us.

This is why we have churches and missionaries who teach about God. He wants us to love Him and others as He loves us.

People that are violent will see in others that violence isn't the way to solve things. Everybody is equal in God's eyes.
*Priscilla Wortman*
*Ms. Lynn's fifth grade class*

One day I was going to the homeless shelter to donate some food. When I got there I realized I did not bring enough food, but I donated what I had and went home. When I got home I found my mom in the kitchen making sandwiches and burgers. When I looked around I saw 15 peanut butter and jelly sandwiches, 15 ham sandwiches, 12 peanut butter and banana sandwiches, 4 hamburgers and 4 cheeseburgers. Then she asked if I wanted to help. I said I would love to. When we were done, in all we made 900 sandwiches in 5 days.

The next day, I took the food to the homeless shelter. They said they love when people give food and clothing to them. When I got home, I asked my mom if we had any clothes that we could give to the homeless shelter. She said that there were two boxes full in the laundry room waiting for me to take to the homeless shelter. So I took the boxes to the homeless shelter. When I arrived there were lots of people eating the food I brought for them earlier. When they saw me they were so excited that I brought clothes for them that they rushed over to me and asked if the clothes were for them. I said they were for them. I put the boxes down and said they could start picking out what clothes they wanted.

Then one of the children came to me when I was leaving and thanked me for the clothing and the food I gave them. After that I went home and went to bed. The next morning when I walked downstairs, I saw that my mom had adopted a baby that was in the shelter, so we got something out of helping the homeless.

*Erin Mock*
*Mrs. Miller's fifth grade class*

When I think of the world today,
People's attitudes seem to reflect "come what may."
People's land and lives are destroyed by the fighting and war.
To this I wish I could say, "Nevermore."
If I could change just one thing,
I would want September 11th memories not to sting.
To be an American is a privilege to me
Because I cherish being free.

*Josh Buttrey*
*Mrs. Miller's fifth grade class*

George Bush is our President. A great guy he is.
He gives poor people dollars and cents.

Boy, if I were president, the things I would do,
Like save the rainforests and trees, too.
I will stop crime and violence
So we can have a happy place to live.

Boy, if I were president, what I would do...
But I will just have to wait until I'm 42!
*Courtney Schaaf*
*Mrs. Miller's fifth grade class*

If I ruled the world, I would help people that were injured on September 11, 2001. I would give people money, clothing and food. I would help people that are paralyzed and need help to get around.
*Brandie Huston*
*Mrs. Miller's fifth grade class*

The world today is at war
Because a jet through the Twin Towers tore.
It was a terrible sight of cowardice and damage.
I was very scared, it was so hard to manage.
What a terrible thing, how could this happen?
I can't believe it. This won't be forgotten.
*Brandon Ellis*
*Mr. Byrd's fifth grade class*

The world around me is so great.
The world around me I cannot hate.
The world around me is so hardy.
The world around me is like a party.
The world around me is so fine.
The world around me I can't define.
The world around me is so safe.
The world around me I trust with faith.
*Lindsey Rutledge*
*Mr. Byrd's fifth grade class*

I would help the community by cleaning up trash, recycling, feeding the homeless people, donating money to schools and charities for victims of the September 11 attacks, and helping the homeless people that do not have homes.

Another way I would help is by building fun stuff like new parks for picnics, fun and exercise. I would add flowers and trees to the parks. I would try to stop people from cutting down the trees.

*Corbin Wieme*
*Mr. Byrd's fifth grade class*

If I ruled the world, the way I would improve it is by making more hospitals, donating money, making world peace and making more room for the forest and animals. The other thing I would do is stop making drugs and alcohol; raise salaries for policemen, firefighters and ambulance drivers; and give homeless people homes as well as end world hunger. People who started fighting would be in big trouble. If we had a war, I would stop it before anyone was killed.

*Corbin Wieme*
*Mr. Byrd's fifth grade class*

If I could change the world, I would demolish all weapons. I would become a better person by thinking before I speak. I would help people by donating money to homeless shelters. I would raise the money by washing cars, selling baked goods and items made by hand. Anyone can change the world. All they have to do is try their hardest.

*Kaitlyn Hargrove*
*Mrs. Hall's fifth grade class*

If I owned the world, I would give homes, food, clothes, and shelter to anyone who needs it. If I owned the world, everyone would be nice. There would be no terrorists or shootings! Stop the stealing and lying. If I owned the world, it would be a peaceful, kind and loving world!

*Brianna Cousins*
*Mrs. Hall's fifth grade class*

If I were a world leader, I would clean the world up. If I were a world leader, I would recycle. If I were a world leader, I would make us all get along. If I were a world leader, I would help anyone who needed help. If I were a world leader, I would give clothes and food to shelters.
*Shelby Gibbs*
*Mrs. Hall's fifth grade class*

If I could change the world, I would stop pollution. To stop pollution, I would make places to put the pollution. Then I would help homeless people in the shelters. I would bring them lots of food and clothes that I do not wear anymore. Next, I would help people who have lost their homes for some reason and help them make more money to buy a home. I would help them find a new job and get more money for them. The last thing I would do to change the world would be to donate money to the homeless and the orphanages.
*Renae Boulogne*
*Mrs. Hall's fifth grade class*

Guns! Guns! Throw away the guns! If you have a gun, then we will send you to an island that has no people and you will never come back. If you do, you are going to jail. Then if you get out of jail, we are going to take you out to the North Pole. We are determined! So no guns!
*Jade Suggs*
*Ms. Lynn's fifth grade class*

Instead of bullets and swords, wars could be fought with paintballs. Each person could get one hundred paintballs. Once they got hit, they would sit on the sideline and watch until five others got out and then they could get back in. This way no one dies and no one gets left out. Everyone wins!
*Kyle Westbrook*
*Ms. Lynn's fifth grade class*

One day I went outside and found a piece of trash. I threw it away because I wanted the world clean. I also recycle everything I can. I even collect any kind of cans I can find. I really am determined to help stomp out litter in my world. Won't you join me?
*Nicholas Meador*
*Ms. Lynn's fifth grade class*

What would you do to help the world? Would you recycle? Could you help the poor get a home? You could work with others to save the environment. Try to save endangered animals. What would *you* do?
*Alyssa Bald*
*Ms. Lynn's fifth grade class*

The world has changed.
It will never be the same.
We have been through a lot of pain.
I wish the world could or would
Get back to the way of God,
Even though the world has changed.
*Nathan Rottero*
*Mrs. Miller's fifth grade class*

On Saturday, five kids started a club to help the world. Every kid in the club came up with an idea to help the world. Jack, the leader of the club, said that he would sail to Africa and teach the people there how to build enormous buildings. Steven, the colonel, said that he would spend every day recycling. Mark, the commander, said that he would fly to Asia and give the kids toys and the adults furniture. Bob, the general, said that he would donate money to people in the world that needed it. Aaron, the captain, said that he would fly to Australia and tell the people to tell other people in other countries to donate things to people that really need it.

So about a week later, the kids gathered up some other friends to go on each of the kids' journeys.

A year later, the five kids met in the clubhouse. They decided that they had helped the world the way they had planned.
*Blake Melton*
*Mrs. Miller's fifth grade class*

The Fightless country is the nicest country there is. No fighting is allowed. If you fight, you get sent to an island where everybody is mean. They always fight and you don't want to go there! But you only stay for a little while. If you fight again, you stay there forever! In the Fightless country, nobody fights and everything is free—houses, apartments, even stores!
*Isaiah Boon*
*Mrs. Miller's fifth grade class*

To save the world, I would go to the Rainforest Café and give money to the rainforest. Did you know that almost all the rainforests are gone? Do you know what a difference we can make in the rainforest? We can save all the trees and animals. Did you know we cannot live without them? We need trees to give us oxygen to breathe and we depend on animals for food. I hope one day I can make a difference in the rainforest. If you want to help, you can make a fund people can donate money to.
*Andrea Stea*
*Mrs. Miller's fifth grade class*

If I ruled I would put an end to terrorism and war. I would recycle aluminum cans and plastic bottles and paper. I would donate money to people in homeless shelters who are sick. I would clean up our community and environment so that people could be healthy. I would donate to churches. I would give kids clothes, shoes and shelter. I would cut the tax bills. I would be a kinder person. So, people, elect me, Aaron Nations.
*Aaron Nations*
*Mr. Byrd's fifth grade class*

Once there was a family named the Tams. They owned a rare garbage can of gold. But this was not an ordinary can. No, it was alive! He was Can Man. When someone was smelling or littering, he was there. He was a world cleaner. He could tell when there was something not clean.

One afternoon a man was stinking up the town. Can Man went over to the man with soap and water. He threw the man inside him and washed him. The man was so happy he hugged Can Man and went home. That's the life of Can Man who kept the world safe for the rest of eternity.

*Seth Owens*
*Mrs. Miller's fifth grade class*

There are two things that I could do to make a difference in the world. First I would help others by donating money, clothes and food. For example, last night my brother and I gave clothes to a family whose apartment burned down. Their dad works with my father.

Last year my New Year's resolution was to donate money to the Red Cross. I did just that last month. I donated $1 to the American Red Cross. I donated money to the people who suffered from the terrorism. I know $1 might not seem a lot, but when you add other peoples' money, it turns into a lot. We are the world. We are the children.

*Brittany Burke*
*Mrs. Hall's fifth grade class*

In today's world there is a lot happening with terrorism. The first thing I would change would be the lives of the poor victims' families. I would raise money and give them clothes and food.

I would also make sure there was no elderly person who was ill or in need of help that was not in a nursing home or a retirement home.

*Brittany Eubanks*
*Mrs. Miller's class fifth grade*

If I ruled the world I would give everybody $500 each. Then I would put everything you can buy down to a dollar. I would put everybody in charge of cleaning the world up. Everybody would be able to go to baseball games, basketball games, hockey games, and any other sports for free. I would really have a good time!
*Bryan Weakly*
*Mrs. Hall's fifth grade class*

I am the future. I will do what's right. I will go to college to get more knowledge. I'll be a teacher and a mother, too. Of course, this will be after I'm married. I'll do the best at my job that I can ever do.

I think that I will be good at my job because I would encourage my students and I would teach them math, reading, spelling, and science.

I don't know if my job will happen, but I hope it does.

It's my dream.
*Alaina Smith*
*Mrs. Brown's third grade class*

# We Are America

I feel so bad about the attack on America. I hope no one does a bad thing again.
*Clarie Brown*
*Mrs. Faoro's first grade class*

I feel sorry that New York had a bad thing happen and the fire.
*Sydney Palmer*
*Mrs. Faoro's first grade class*

We are all free
In the land of the free.
We are the brave,
This is what we will rave.
We will all fight,
And we will unite.
Our eagle will soar,
While the Taliban is sore!
If our soldiers die,
Then we will cry.
We will fight
With all our might.
Osama bin Laden, you better watch out.
Our men will get you, without a doubt.
When it's all over and you see red, white and blue,
Remember America. We did this for you!
*Taylor Thompson*
*Mrs. Brown's third grade class*

Children aren't taking the Pledge of Allegiance seriously. People of our nation are fighting for our country in Afghanistan. America should make sure that people take the Pledge of Allegiance seriously. The pledge is more than something you do every day. It's something you do for your country.

*Dedicated to Glen Stone*

*Javin Stone*
*Mrs. Brown's third grade class*

I think that I'm very lucky to live in America because we get lots of food to eat and we're safe. There are lots of nice people. There are stores and lots of places to have fun. We have beds to sleep in and homes to live in. There are schools so you can learn. There are places for you to go out and eat. There are places where you can work. There are libraries where you can get books. There are lots of comfort. You're free to do lots of things.
*Ali Isham*
*Ms. Ladas' third grade class*

I like our country. I hope the war ends soon. I want everyone to stop fighting. I want my cousin who is fighting in the war to come back from the war. I hope you don't drink and drive. I hope you are good in this country and do good things. I hope you respect our country.
*Robert Garrott*
*Mrs. Laster's third grade class*

If we could make a time machine, we could go to September 10, 2001 and tell the President to shut down all airports so the terrorists from Afghanistan could not destroy the Twin Towers. Then we would not have to worry about terrorists attacking the United States and the taking our country from us.
*Kelley Lynn*
*Mrs. Bennett's fourth grade class*

On September 11, 2001 there was a plane that hit the Twin Towers and caused a big fire. I wish the terrorists could see what they did to me. I didn't know this would be such a tragedy for me. I wish there were no terrorists because they make my life miserable. That was the day my life changed.
*Jared Prall*
*Mrs. Hall's fifth grade class*

One day a man had the nerve to knock down our Twin Towers. He may take away our Towers, but he can't take away our freedom. On that sad day, everyone in New York was heartbroken and sad. Osama bin Laden can't take away our pride. It was a sad day for the people who were innocently working when this happened. This attack made history, but still it does not take away our pride and joy.
*Dustin Garcia*
*Mr. Byrd's fifth grade class*

What happened on September 11 has changed my tomorrow.
The 11th was a day of pain and sorrow.
That attack has hurt the United States badly,
Many people lost their lives or a loved one sadly.
Still, America has pulled through, "United We Stand."
I am sad for the innocent people on the planes that didn't land.
Bin Laden will be captured for his awful prank,
For in the aftermath our hearts sank.
And he cannot stop the *United* States of America!
*Shelby Hall*
*Mr. Byrd's fifth grade class*

The Twin Towers once stood tall,
But the terrorists tried to take it all.
We, as Americans, stand proud and true,
God bless America, and God bless you.

We are Americans, bold and free,
Together we stand, you and me.
All I want is to be free.
Proud people gave that right to me.
*Shane House*
*Mr. Byrd's fifth grade class*

So many things you can see,
America and me.
Lots of things you want to be,
America and me.
America is like a tree,
Growing beneath me.
America and me.
*Tara Reece*
*Mr. Byrd's fifth grade class*

This is my country! I sing it with pride.
I remember the men that fought for it and died.
It is my duty to keep it clean.
When I see someone litter it makes one want to scream.
I tell them, "We need to keep the earth clean for our future,
so pick up your litter and be mature."
Just remember you can make the world different.
Just be on the lookout for someone who wants to pull
a quick stunt.
*Rebekah Patton*
*Mrs. Hall's fifth grade class*

We are the world. We are the children. We are the U.S.A. We are the 50 strong states. We are the people. We receive treasures from up above. We have the freedom to do what's good or bad. We can believe in what we want. We are proud to be Americans.
*Brittany Todoroff*
*Ms. Lynn's fifth grade class*

In the past we have had some wars.
Can you tell me what they were for?
Just to protect our freedom.
Now our country is at war.
Can you tell me what it is for?
Just to protect our freedom.
When I grow up, what can I be to protect our liberty?
Be a man of God.
*Jack Singleton*
*Ms. Lynn's fifth grade class*

We are united. We are the world. We can make a difference if we try. We can hold hands and work together as a team. We are unstoppable. Lift your hands up and tell it to the world.
*Dasha Hatcher*
*Ms. Lynn's fifth grade class*

We are the United States of America. The people of America are sad because we were attacked on September 11, 2001. More than 3,000 American people were killed. Now we are hurt in our hearts, but we are not hurt in our minds. We are angry, mad, and wanting to get revenge on the man that hurt America. People are still sad about what happened. The American people have overcome the attacks. Now the American soldiers are bombing the people that are responsible for this destruction. I know we will get over this, but we will not forget in our hearts.
*Audrey Joines*
*Mr. Byrd's fifth grade class*

We stand proud of the United States. Remember the September 11th attack on America. There were a lot of innocent children left orphaned from the September 11, 2001 attack. Now we're trying to get peace. Since September 11, there has been no peace at all. We struck back at Osama bin Laden, but we have not gotten him yet. Now we kids are donating one dollar to the children of Afghanistan. We're going to try to get peace back.
*Chris Fleming*
*Ms. Lynn's fifth grade class*

# When I Grow Up

When I grow up I want to be an army man. I'm going to go far away on a big ship.
*Nicholas Biggers*
*Mrs. Tuggle's kindergarten class*

When I grow up I want to be a police officer. I would arrest the people that hurt other people. I would help people that help other people. I would help people that need to go to the hospital.
*Dannah Roberts*
*Mrs. Tuggle's kindergarten class*

When I grow up I want to be a sister and a bride. I would help my brother and share wonderful games. I want to be a bride dressed in purple and light candles at the church.
*Catherine Crunk*
*Mrs. Tuggle's kindergarten class*

When I grow up I want to be a football player for the Steelers. I would be nice and not make any fouls.
*Preston Reed*
*Mrs. Tuggle's kindergarten class*

When I grow up I want to be a dad because I like children. I will work at the newspaper. I will cook for my children on my day off.
*Parker Brandon*
*Mrs. Tuggle's kindergarten class*

When I grow up I want to be an army man. I would be in a tank and shoot. I would save the world from bad guys.
*Garret Mudd*
*Mrs. Tuggle's kindergarten class*

When I grow up I want to be a firefighter just like my dad. I would save people and put out fires.
*Austin Inglish*
*Mrs. Tuggle's kindergarten class*

When I grow up I want to be a science teacher. I would show kids how to do experiments. I would invent a robot dog that could do whatever we want it to.
*Issac Maxey*
*Mrs. Tuggle's kindergarten class*

When I grow up I'm going to be a mom. I will take care of two children. I will clean my house and make it look pretty.
*Yasmine El-Chaer*
*Mrs. Tuggle's kindergarten class*

# My Name Is

My name is Ashley. I love my mom. I can hop.
*Ashley McCutheon*
*Mrs. West's kindergarten class*

My name is Beau. I love rabbits. I can play my video games.
*Beau Booth*
*Mrs. West's kindergarten class*

My name is Reanna. I love flowers and I can ride my bike.
*Reanna Knight*
*Mrs. West kindergarten class*

My name is Tyus. I love Mom and Dad. I can ride my bike.
*Tyus Jobe*
*Mrs. West's kindergarten class*

My name is Cameron. I love my bike. I can ride my scooter.
*Cameron Schaaf*
*Mrs. West's kindergarten class*

My name is Tyler. I love my puppy. I can play corner.
*Tyler Rogers*
*Mrs. West's kindergarten class*

My Name is Kristen. I love Mommy and Daddy. I can ride my bike.
*Kristen Price*
*Mrs. West's kindergarten class*

My name is Matthew. I love Mom and Dad. I can ride my bike.
*Matthew Sanford*
*Mrs. West's kindergarten class*

My name is Abby. I love Mom and Dad. I can play ball.
*Ashley Loring*
*Mrs. West's kindergarten class*

My name is Tasha. I love Mistye. I can be brush my teeth.
*Tasha Crosser*
*Mrs. West's kindergarten class*

My name is Mike. I love Mom and Dad. I can ride my bike.
*Mike Murrell*
*Mrs. West's kindergarten class*

My name is Rachel. I am 6 years old. I wish my dog Goochie were still alive. She could sleep with me and she wouldn't hurt other dogs that were puppies. I like the Christmas holiday best of all. I am happiest when I go to my nana's house.
*Rachel Williams*
*Mrs. Taylor's first grade class*

My name is Eric. I am six years old. I wish I could go to France to see what it looks like and play with the boys and girls there. Football is my favorite sport. I like to eat vanilla ice cream, mostly in the summer time. It is yummy! If I had just one wish I would like a new puppy.
*Eric Hughes*
*Mrs. Taylor's first grade class*

My name is Joshua and I am six years old. I like to play volleyball and my favorite books are about bears. The black bears are best.
*Joshua Wormer*
*Mrs. Taylor's first grade class*

My name is Kyle and I am seven years old. I like to play all kinds of sports games and backward hide-and-seek too. My favorite time of the year is our family Christmas in St. Louis, Missouri. All twelve of my cousins go there. We get to swim at the hotel pool and get presents from GranMother and GranDaddy. My favorite part about school is playing. I love America but sometimes bad people do bad things. I can give my love to the world so maybe bad people won't be bad. Earth is a great planet for me.
*Kyle Martinelli*
*Mrs. Taylor's first grade class*

My name is Brandon and I am six years old. My teacher thinks she would not have a Kimodo dragon for a pet like I do. It's a lizard. I would keep it in my room in a glass cage. I don't know what it likes to eat. I like to read the Dr. Seuss books. He writes funny books. Boys and girls everywhere know about Dr. Seuss.
*Brandon O'Rear*
*Mrs. Taylor's first grade class*

My name is Ashley. I am six years old. I really love reading at school. I am in first grade and I got to read to my kindergarten teacher. That was fun. I learn lots of things about boys and girls around the world when I read. We are studying about boys and girls in Germany, Mexico, Spain and Sweden. They like to play and do some of the same things as me. I think I would like to go to Spain.
*Ashley Eldridge*
*Mrs. Taylor's first grade class*

My name is Rebecca. I am six years old but I am very tall. Maybe someday I can play basketball. I have three big dogs and I like to play with them. Boys and girls in other lands like to play with dogs too. I wish I could go see some boys and girls around the world. We could play and be friends.
*Rebecca Garrott*
*Mrs. Taylor's first grade class*

My name is Neal. I am seven years old. I really like the summertime because I love to swim and ride the four-wheelers at my aunt's house. I like Christmas time a lot too. I wish it were already Christmas. We are going to help some little boy or girl who does not have as much as I do. All boys and girls everywhere need lots of love.
*Neal Cothron*
*Mrs. Taylor's first grade class*

My name is Brett. I am six years old. I like it when my friends come over. This is when I am happiest. My favorite books are about Harry Potter and I really like my brother's computer game about Harry Potter. I like to play with my dog Rudy outside a lot.
*Brett Smith*
*Mrs. Taylor's first grade class*

My name is Amber Myers. I love Mom and Dad. I like to play with my cat.
*Amber Myers*
*Mrs. Buttrey's first grade class*

My name is Rylie. I want a trampoline. I like my cousin. I like to watch T.V.
*Rylie Clairday*
*Mrs. Buttrey's first grade class*

My name is Emily. I am thankful for my mommy.
*Emily Cross*
*Mrs. Buttrey's first grade class*

My name is Austin. We won our baseball championship.
*Austin Nichols-Hurst*
*Mrs. Buttrey's first grade class*

My name is Katriel Coleman. My dad, my brother and I built a workbench. I ran into the garbage can.
*Katriel Coleman*
*Mrs. Buttrey's first grade class*

My name is Michaela and I love God.
*Michaela Webb*
*Mrs. Buttrey's first grade class*

My name is Bryson Hutchison. I like to watch T.V. I like Dragon Ball Z.
*Bryson Hutchison*
*Mrs. Buttrey's first grade class*

My name is Lexi Emilia. I love my friends. A friend is someone you play with. I am a girl that loves my family.
*Lexi Emilia*
*Mrs. Buttrey's first grade class*

My name is Blake Word. I am responsible for my brother and sister. I am thankful for food.
*Blake Word*
*Mrs. Buttrey's first grade class*

My name is Dillion Kruppa. I think Cooper is very smart. I have a cast.
*Dillion Kruppa*
*Mrs. Buttrey's first grade class*

My name is Steven. I like my friends.
*Steven York*
*Mrs. Faoro's first grade class*

My name is Dillion. I love school. It is fun.
*Dillion Eakes*
*Mrs. Faoro's first grade class*

My name is Dalton. I like to play outside every day. I like to play tag.
*Dalton Taylor*
*Mrs. Faoro's first grade class*

My name is Candis Corley. I like to ride my bike with my friends.
*Candis Corley*
*Mrs. Buttrey's first grade class*

My name is James Taylor White. I like to play basketball. I know how to shoot the ball. I know how to pass the ball.
*James Taylor White*
*Mrs. Buttrey's first grade class*

My name is Morgan Meade. I am responsible for my room. I am responsible for my living room.
*Morgan Meade*
*Mrs. Buttrey's first grade class*

My name is Bethany Stansell. I love Mama and my Dad and my brothers and my grandparents.
*Bethany Stansell*
*Mrs. Buttrey's first grade class*

My name is Avery-Ana. I am six years old. I have a pet rabbit and his name is Sparkplug. I have to feed him in the morning before I go to school and at night. Sometimes I wish I had some baby rabbits too, but Mom and Dad say that would be too many animals.
*Avery-Ana Green*
*Mrs. Taylor's first grade class*

My name is Joe. I am six years old. My birthday is the day before Christmas. I am happiest when I am with my mom and play hide-and-seek inside. We have fun. I like to hide under the bed. I wish all boys and girls could have fun with their moms too.
*Joe Cottles*
*Mrs. Taylor's first grade class*

My name is Laura. I would like to have a trampoline. I want to be in tap dancing.
*Laura Bell*
*Mrs. Buttrey's first grade class*

My name is Mackenzie. I love the world. It's a blastoff. All of us love the world. It's amazing.
*Mackenzie Wright*
*Mrs. Pryor's second grade class*

My name is Kaitlyn Lawrence. I am in the third grade. My school is so cool. We are nice. We are the world. We have fun at school. We are a cool school. We are not bad. We hate drugs. We love God. We are cool at school.
*Kaitlyn Lawrence*
*Mrs. Brown's third grade class*

# Acrostics

**R**utland Elementary School.
**E**ducation.
**S**howing respect.
**P**eople who care will join.
**E**xcellent! I'm all ready in the group.
**C**ongratulations, Rutland, you won
**T**he trophy!
*Elle Bray*
*Mrs. VanCleve second grade class*

**R**utland is nice to
**E**veryone in the world.
**S**cholastic news are neat
**P**apers and some are on computers too.
**E**veryone treats people nicely!
**C**ool things are in here
**T**oday and every day!
*Cassie Bean*
*Mrs. VanCleve's second grade class*

**R**utland
**E**ducation
**S**elf-esteem
**P**eople that care
**E**xceptional
**C**aring
**T**eachers who love us
*Lance Highers*
*Mrs. VanCleve's second grade class*

**R** is for respect.
**E** is for education.
**S** is for success.
**P** is for the pledge.
**E** is for excellent teaching.
**C** is for interesting classes.
**T** is for nice teachers.
*Lakota Smith*
*Mrs. VanCleve's second grade class*

**R** is for Rutland and it's the best!
**E** is for everyone here. We know we are the best.
**S** is for school and I like it a lot.
**P** is for the people in this school.
**E** is for everyone who is excellent.
**C** is for cannot. We know better than that.
**T** is for try. We do that a lot and we will never stop.
*Emlie Carmon*
*Mrs. VanCleve's second grade class*

**R**utland is
**E**xciting
**S**pecial teachers
**P**eople
**E**ating in the room with Mrs. VanCleve
**C**aring for others
**T**rustworthy throughout the day
*Travis Madewell*
*Mrs. VanCleve's second grade class*

**R**utland is a very big school.
**E**lementary means young children.
**S**chool is a place you go to learn.
**P**eople who help are helpers.
**E**xcellent makes perfect.
**C**aring is helpful.
**T**he room is big.
*Brandon Boyd*
*Mrs. VanCleve's second grade class*

**R**espect Rutland
**E**lementary School
**S**tudents help teach
**P**eople do too.
**E**xciting books
**C**aring people
**T**aking turns
*Carly Johns*
*Mrs. VanCleve's second grade class*

**R**utland Rockets
**E**lementary
**S**chool success
**P**ay attention
**E**xcellent handwriting
**C**aring people
**T**rustworthiness is to trust somebody
*Preston Young*
*Mrs. VanCleve's second grade class*

**R**utland is the best school
**E**verybody's reading
**S**pecial—that's what I am
**P**ledge allegiance to the flag
**E**lementary school is cool
**C**aring for people
**T**eachers are the best
*Edrika Santiago*
*Mrs. VanCleve's second grade class*

**R**utland Elementary is fun.
**E**veryone loves school
**S**ocial studies is cool.
**P**lease help others.
**E**lementary school is a great place.
**C**aring is what teachers do.
**T**rustworthiness is nice.
*Jonathon Culbert*
*Mrs. VanCleve's second grade class*

**R**ain
**A**pple
**C**ooking
**H**appy
**A**thletic
**E**xploring
**L**oves learning

**K**ind
**E**xtra special
**I**ce cream
**S**andwich
**L**ibrary
**I**ce-skating
**N**ice
**G**ame Boy Advance
*Rachel Keisling*
*Mrs. Rowland's CDC class*

**A**ctive
**L**eaping
**E**ating
**C**amping

**H**appy
**E**nergetic
**P**izza
**B**usy
**U**nique
**R**ambunctious
**N**ature
*Alec Hepburn*
*Mrs. Rowland's CDC class*

**D**rum
**A**ctive
**V**ideos
**I**nteresting
**D**rawing

**R**unning
**O**utside
**D**ancing
**R**est time
**I**mportant
**G**ames
**U**nique
**E**at
**Z**ippidee-do-dah
*David Rodriguez*
*Mrs. Rowland's CDC class*

**D**inosaur
**U**nderstanding
**A**pplesauce
**N**ice
**E**nergetic

**C**ute
**H**elpful
**U**nique
**R**unning
**C**hocolate pie
**H**eart
*Duane Church*
*Mrs. Rowland's CDC class*

**D**octor
**O**ptimistic
**M**annerly
**I**nteresting
**N**eat
**I**mportant
**Q**uick
**U**nique
**E**xceptional

**D**rum
**A**ctive
**V**ideos
**I**n love
**S**uper
*Dominique Davis*
*Mrs. Rowland's CDC class*

**B** is for buddies!
**E** is for enjoying.
**S** is for best friends' secrets.
**T** is for thankful friends.

**F** is for friends.
**R** is for really cool friends.
**I** is for interesting friends.
**E** is for energetic friends.
**N** is for nice friends.
**D** is for devoted friends.
**S** is for special friends.
*Hanna Carr*
*Mrs. Brown's third grade class*

**C**hildren are special to the world.
**H**e or she can be special if they are nice.
**I** can be special if I am nice to other people.
**L**et all the children be nice to each other.
**D**rugs make people not be nice.
*Austin Brown*
*Mrs. Brown's third grade class*

**D**rugs are bad!
**R**eading let's us know they are bad.
**U**sing your brain will keep you from doing them.
**G**iving out drugs is bad.

**F**iguring out not to do them is smart.
**R**emembering to just say no is wise.
**E**ating good food, not pills, is best.
**E**ncouraging people not to use drugs will help our world.
*Ashley Gabrielle*
*Mrs. Brown's third grade class*

**L** is for children who love to play.
**O** is for oceans that rest.
**V** is for how they are violet.
**E** is for east where many live.

**I** is for God I trust.
**N** is for newborn.

**T** is for the children who love Jesus.
**H** is for the heart that loves you.
**E** is for everyone being treated equally.

**W** is for where all people are free.
**O** is for on the real world where there are a lot of children.
**R** is for really great children
**L** is for love that all people have.
**D** is for decorations of love.
*Stephanie Davis*
*Mrs. Cardwell's fourth grade class*

**O**ur home
**U**nited States
**R**espect

**N**ational holidays
**A**nthem
**T**eamwork
**I**ndependent
**O**ne God
**N**avy
*Brandon Ray*
*Mrs. Bennett's fourth grade class*

**W**ritings
**O**rganizations
**R**eligions
**L**ove
**D**ome
'**S**trong

**F**ree
**R**isk
**E**ducation
**D**ecisions
**O**ur rights
**M**ighty
*Aaron Moss*
*Mr. Byrd's fifth grade class*

# Friendship

My best friend is Seth Carey. We invite each other to play and spend the night. He's silly like me but sometimes he's serious. He ripped Mikey Brown's underwear.

My other best friend is Mikey Brown. He likes nachos. He talks tacos and burritos. He says "chickens." He is silly all the time.

My other best friend is Austin Dodd. He's not silly mostly. He likes to sing the "doom song." He lives a block away from me.

My other best friend is Austin Brown. He's silly sometimes. He likes Florida. He lives across the street from his church.

Friends, you can have more than one.

*Jacob Everett*
*Mrs. Brown's third grade class*

Friendship is something we all need. I have lots of friends. Some of my friends are Maggie, Alaina, Melissa, and Zach H. Some of my friends I've known all my life. Others I have just met in school or church. My friends are important to me because they are kind, they make me laugh, and more.

*Rachel Grindstaff*
*Mrs. Brown's third grade class*

I have more than one best friend. I think that some people try to make you think you can have only one best friend. But I think all of our friends should be our best friends. All of my friends are my best friends. All of my friends are cool. Their names are Schaffer, Cameron, Javin, Ryan, Austin Brown, Austin Dodd, Kyle Elliott, Kyle Illgen, Carson, and Mikey.

Schaffer's favorite subject is spelling. Cameron's favorite subject is math. Javin's favorite subject is social studies. Ryan's favorite subject is science. Austin Brown's favorite subject is math. Austin Dodd's favorite subject is science. Kyle Elliot's favorite subject is math. Kyle Illegen's favorite subjects are science and math. Those are my friends and their favorite subjects. Even though we have different favorite subjects, we are still best friends.

*David Putman*
*Mrs. Brown's third grade class*

Everybody needs friends! I have friends. You have friends. If the world didn't have friends everybody would be bored on the weekends. And there are a whole bunch of other ways that people would be bored. Some people think you can only have only one friend. I don't believe that. My best friends are David and Cameron. David's favorite color is green to and his favorite subject is math. I like my friends. They're cool! I like them a lot. I hope I'm a good friend.

*Ryan Clairday*
*Mrs. Brown's third grade class*

My friend David Putman's favorite pet is an anaconda. His favorite sport is baseball. His best friends are Cameron and me. He's about 4' 1". He sits by Kassity. David likes to read. We can do the worm. His favorite color is green. He's my best friend. Friends make the world better because if we all hated each other we'd be fighting all the time.

*Mikey Brown*
*Mrs. Brown's third grade class*

This summer I met was a kid named Jacob. He moved close to me in August. After about a month, he and I had become best friends. One day he told me he was looking for a church. I told him he was welcome at my church. After a while he came to my church for a couple of Sundays. He and his mom started to get used to my church. They stayed, got saved and baptized, and started coming to my church every Sunday.
*Joey Patterson*
*Ms. Ladas' third grade class*

Friendship, friendship all around, from the top to the ground. Friendship is a special thought that spreads to the children of the world.
*Maggie Thornton*
*Ms Ladas' third grade class*

# Menagerie

## Roses Are Red

Roses are red,
Violets are blue,
You are sweet
And I am too.
*Dallas Karr*
*Mrs. Faoro's first grade class*

## Roses Are Red

Roses are red.
Violets are blue.
I wish you
Had one too!
*Keanna Illgen*
*Mrs. Faoro's first grade class*

## Wacko

I don't smoke or take drugs. Drugs are not good for your body. Neither is smoking. Tobacco is wacko!
*Carson Reddick*
*Mrs. Brown's third grade class*

## Smelly Feet

My sister's feet smell like meat,
My brother said they are sweet.
She stomps her feet to the beat,
And makes it sound really neat.
My mom tells her to get out of the street,
To come to the table and take her seat.
If you clean your plate when you eat,
I will let you all have a treat.
*Hannah Grace Carr*
*Mrs. Brown's third grade class*

## My Cat Pat

I have an orange cat.
He lies on a mat
And he eats big, fat rats.
He has a red hat.
His name is Pat.
That's my cat.
*Kassity Shepherd*
*Mrs. Brown's third grade class*

## The Drawing Poem

I like to draw and hang my pictures on the wall.
I hope one day they do not fall.
If they do, my mom will hang them in the hall.
*Cameron Cheatham*
*Mrs. Brown's third grade class*

## Skiing in Sun

Skiing is exciting and very fun.
I like to ski in the sun.
I like it a ton.
*Carson Reddick*
*Mrs. Brown's third grade class*

## What I See

I see a star,
It is very far.
I see a flipper
Near a zipper.
I see a dragon
In a wagon.
I see a boat.
Most of them float.
*Allison Hulsey*
*Mrs. Brown's third grade class*

## The Deer in the Snow

I saw the prettiest thing today.
It was a deer leaping away,
Over a fence and into the snow.
Far away she did go.
*Melissa Woodruff*
*Mrs. Brown's third grade class*

## What I Love to Do

I love to write,
I love the sight.

I love the tub,
I love to rub.

I love to cook.
I love to read a book.

But most of all I love too much!
*Sharahd Stinson*
*Mr. Marczak's third grade class*

## My Baby Sister

My baby sister is really swell.
I love her smile but not her smell.
She likes to throw stuff at the wall,
But most of all her favorite ball.
When her diaper's dirty, she smells like squash,
And then my mom gives her a wash.
*AJ Schultz*
*Mr. Marczak's third grade class*

## The Planets Poem

The planets poem
The planets poe
The planets po
The planets p
The planets
The planet
The plane
The plan
The pla
The pl
The p
The
Th
T
Where are all of the planets?
*Danielle Chaffin*
*Ms. Ladas' third grade class*

## Santa

Santa comes tonight
On the busiest flight.
He huffs and puffs all through the night
Till you see him on his next flight.
*Linsey Ward*
*Ms. Ladas' third grade class*

## Say No to Drugs

I'm drug-free and so are you. Let's be drug-free all the way through. I am not having drugs for me, no way! So just get them away from me. I am not taking any drugs because drugs can really mess up your brain. Wear your drug-free ribbon all the time. Keep it on until you're in college. When you're in college, wear the red ribbon until you're 20.
*Schaffer Palmer*
*Mrs. Brown's third grade class*

## My One Special Day

My team was playing a tough game. I was up to bat, three balls, two strikes, when BOOM! I hit the ball hard. The ball hit the fence. This has been a good year so far.
*Kyle Elliott*
*Mrs. Brown's third grade class*

## Roses Are Red

Roses are red, violets are nice. America is too. So are people if you are nice to them.
*Collin Sullivan*
*Ms. Ladas' third grade class*

## My Cat

My cat is so fat.
All he does is lie on his mat.
He never catches a rat.
My cat is so fat
His fat hangs over his mat.
*Steve Workman*
*Ms. Ladas' third grade class*

## In My School

In my school it's very nice. Mrs. Kittrell is the principal. She is nice. So are the teachers like Mrs. Miller, Mrs. Hall, and don't forget Mrs. Brown. She's my homeroom teacher. One of the teachers is my mom. She's the resource teacher. There are a whole lot more teachers, but I don't know all them.
*Allison Hulsey*
*Mrs. Brown's third grade class*

## Deep Inside

Deep inside my dog's doghouse,
There's stuff to be found.
Maybe there's a bone or a jar of fleas.
Deep inside, my dog is waiting for me.
Deep inside, my dog is ferocious so I don't go too deep.
There is something, however, that I do know:
Chihuahuas don't like to be disturbed!
*David Mays*
*Mr. Marczak's third grade class*

## The Mystery of Peace

One early morning, I got up and saw my brother eating my candy bar! "What are you doing?!" I yelled at my brother. "Eating," he said. "Eat this!" "Boys!" said my mom. "Yes, ma'am?" I said, stopping my clenched fist which was about to pound my brother. "Why can't you get along and have peace?" And that gave me an idea. I ran off into my backyard. I looked around and found it! It was my Indian peace pipe. I picked it up, and on the bottom was a peace sign. It started to glow! "Holy..." I said. My brother and mother came outside. "Whoa!" my brother said. "Is it safe?" "I don't know, but I'll see." I put it on and all of a sudden everything was glowing! "Whoa!" I said. Then everything was back to normal and peaceful. Even my brother and I never fought again, nor anyone else in the world. I think I found world peace! I'm looking for that pipe again, just in case I need it.
*Willie Todd*
*Mr. Byrd's fifth grade class*

## The Giving

One day I was walking down the street.
I gave someone something good to eat.
He asked me the time,
Because he couldn't read his watch due to the grime.
I gave him my watch to replace the old.
His smile glistened like gold.
He said "Thank you, sir"
And the rest was a blur.
*Sean Kirkpatrick*
*Mrs. Hall's fifth grade class*

## Looking for Glory

I'm simply a poet, I don't want to blow it.
I was trained by a guy who was nothing but shy.
I can rhyme all the time 'cause it ain't no crime.
Now that is my story—I am looking for glory.
*Josh Buttrey*
*Mrs. Miller's fifth grade class*

## Message in a Bottle

On a sunny day at a beach, three kids found a message in a bottle. It said, "We, the children of the world." So that very day, they brought it back to their own personal club. The next day they decided to go on a voyage around the world. So they gathered a million kids. The mayor was very pleased.

The next day, they were very excited to know that their trip would begin. It took them five years and 120 days, but one glorious day, every kid stood around the world and the three kids that planned this said, "Everybody shout, *'WE ARE THE WORLD! WE ARE THE CHILDREN!'*" Everyone on earth could hear! It was marvelous! So remember: *"We are the world! We are the children!"*

*William Mackie*
*Mrs. Miller's fifth grade class*

## Dreams

Dreams can be BIG.
Dreams can be small.
You can dream of American people,
Standing tall.

Dreams can be good.
Dreams can be bad.
September 11th was like a dream
That was very, very sad.

Dreams can be short.
Dreams can be long.
In America, you can make your dreams come true.
Thanks to the red, white and blue.
*Kristen Madewell*
*Mrs. Miller's fifth grade class*

## I Would Say No

Just say no?
Just say no!
Just say no
To drugs!
No way!
Just say no?
Just say no!
Just say no
To violence!
Just say yes?
Just say yes!
Just say yes
To kind caring!
Say *yes*!
*Amie Vanderpool*
*Ms. Lynn's fifth grade class*

## The Future

I look in the future and what do I see?
Am I a grownup? Am I as tall as can be?
Wars and bombs are going on, hitting countries like
one, two, three.
Yet we wish it will stop, we want to be free.
United we stand, divided we fall.
We are the children, love each and all.
Remember we are the world and we all stand tall.
*Preston Jenkins*
*Mr. Byrd's fifth grade class*

## I See

Here I am walking around
Seeing people on the streets.
I see homeless people.
I see busy and "in a hurry" people.
I see people getting out of cars.
I see people going to work.
We live in a busy world.
Sometimes we are too busy to help others.
But after September 11, we all changed.
We now take time to help people.
So I see caring people.
I see helping people.
I see all different races working together.
I see the U.S.A.
*Brandon Kemp*
*Mr. Byrd's fifth grade class*

Printed in the United States
4343

9 781931 718295